in ghostly onehead

J. D. NELSON

Dec. 2023
Pax tecum sit.
JDNelson

Post-Asemic Press 021

Library of Congress Control Number: 2022950874

ISBN: 978-1-7366147-3-0

Postasemicpress.wordpress.com
Postasemicpress.blogspot.com
Contact: postasemicpress@gmail.com

Cover design by Michael Jacobson

Cover image by George Hodan
"Cellarium at Fountains Abbey"
North Yorkshire, England

For the Nelson kids, with love.

Foreword

J. D. Nelson presents a harvest of lines that you wish you'd thought of. More than that, he gathers them up & presents them in a succession of poems you wish that you'd written. It's a jealous wish, though, because nobody can shape a poem like J. D. can.

He's a variety of things all gathered together in a compact whole, & he owns it. "I've won this earth / I'm wording it this way." Acrobat, surrealist, rapper, sociologist, mountain-top purveyor of enlightenment, hermit in his underground laboratory. & that's just with his poetry! He carries on a permanent conversation with the world itself, &, at the same time, maintains a spellcasting commentary on the interchange for the rest of us. If he can't find the word that fits then he'll invent one; & the world — & us along with it — smile at his wisdom & we all feel the better for it.

—Mark Young, poet, artist, and editor, 5.1.21

I

the aurorae in here

on a brown paper towel
the tv screen ammonia

the dream-diamond shape
study your maps — are you a crow?

the burton *hernie*, the embery
(time is a thumb stomach)

sleep ok?
the news is wooden & weird

now is the ugly time for game shows
mr. pizza machine

the detroit rock! rock! liver

o woolen moon
yes, bug!

this calm strube day
this fruit punch red

the coy volume cabot
earth, yes!

nice restaurants, traditionally
the water's free, huh?

this is the frontal bread
the faint "coo, coo" of the mourning dove

a daylight poem

I've been growing all night

    in the dark
    in my sleep

the gamble of *sharking* the chain-chimney
you must show proof of potato ownership

half-hulk
cobwebs (that old trouble)

    this one toe
    the doc rips

the wrong book
the stolen broken

this is the serious pine

the good grady in the suit & tie
the good glass arrow & the panther after

tonight's film:
the chris & chris finish

      a violin hat!

experience earth in your skin-suit!
I said, "clean eyes"

laughing into my hoof
I am the ox with human feet

someone hums
hum-m-m

scoop vs. ump

another thinking
machine machine machine

I'm the one with tanned eyes
soup for the lonely world

this is the meaning
this is the cotton of the sparkle

the gulf helpers
the dry soup mix

tonight is the worm
to be needed at a target store

the sanka coffee angel to go

a green spinach hat
a marlboro mask

a batch of bats
following the fox

the thinking brain
one *chrono* of itself

earth is the self
needing the skull for one day only

now the earth bursts
the moon of that

the law is the lapper
the nap now

the water water

wooden water is the start
after the thoughts

police nectar and salt
earth is the water

needing a water sock
the western west

reed one to thaw the old wet rinse
news of the rye football

      closing another bank account at midnight
      the same meal plan for days and days and days

the last of the sea foam
the help is the thinking cube

this wolf is the woolly wol'

the prime lime
the cold earth

there's no money in it
the sink is barely alive

the wishing mushroom
together together

the spider tapping
this is me, needing myself

this is the gumshoe
the rapping potato

the smart health apple

777 = the golden knot
too much space bar

in my football field boots
too heavy for the world

standing with the brain
looking for the light

a famous tiger
is that the plaid in pants?

when I am a machine
a tree on the beach

the fright of the cloud-man
the dripping sun

space now

earth has the money, all right
the tree is hatching

the spaced-out cop
the soul cop

a friend is in the boat
I could say not to talk

I'm in the blue boots
here comes the red fox in the rowboat

without the sun now

for your forest and that dried-up lake

this one is the color tv version

this one is the world, and that self is here with the light

this one is the normal help, and that sand is the challenge
to learn of it here

this one is the truck when cooling the boat

this one is the face, and that corner is the chain
with the american name

this one is learning that time is a wheel and the eye now

     time to begin with the new colors, and I get it

the coin serf

is that the same thing as the ape space, the outer space?
taking a class and knowing something [flim-flam, flu]

a fool for the trees
this is the friend of a friend I was telling you about

salt to warn the oatmeal
a brown bottle of root beer

now tux
the elvis level

longmont, south of downtown

waiting for the bus on the side of the highway
squatting, eating cheeseburgers from a paper bag

what ever happened to the kerouac gas station?

a strange apple or nelson popcorn

      888

a pile of pie!
noon in on it

the light show and the charm of the pattern

the sun ate a little more of the grass
"this is some good grass," said the sun

this one is the light blue sun, named fredo
blue nacho chips, and so on

nothing is the sun
nothing one two is three

is this the star and the start?
the food is wet

a little door for my feet

looking thru cookbooks
looking at the book of kings and queens

faster than the color of the cuckoo
the yellow makes the clock

some of the brighter sun was felt here, too
        you mean that little green sun?
yeah, that thing

        I know, man — it is the worst
                no, you guys, it's cool
        no way
                yeah, it is

earth is the almond

some of the book will be about the look of the sunlight
the clean chair means clean sitting

you wish for something else
but it is bread and bread and bread

when thinking & *tarking*
nothing here is the color of the mind

what are we losing?
that same old wet scram set

chairlift seasoning
be aware of the smithy

Ө_Ө

when the morn becomes brittle
the brain is surprised to "see" anything

     innsbruck now
     already alaska

we had a little sock out back
that old earth with old heads

the backs of my hands burn
the first *urfing* in years

I am the blinking clown
(with the cheddar hair)

word that *lerd*
or is it *lurred*?

the brain of the wild bee

red earth has the law
the wheelbarrow earth

this is the finishing cough — no touching!
the wood and water spirit

the old tank of goldfish

room for that pirate cake
a slow chirp

something made with hands or brains
this trick in a roman cloud

the clown cloud car
one scrambled

egg mtn — how is it?
earth was swallowed up by a space worm

don't look for the answer in crab sand

when I get back with the paper sun
earth will receive a red medal

the leader of the moths
the snow apple

raft after
you need that multi for better gamma

cuts on my hands from puppy teeth
I become the wolf

a peace video with corn seed
from the pond to the sun

the final eye on toast

dear bread,
listen to me, bread!

this stripe finalizes it
this is the feather of the caramel hoist

I'm reading the book as I'm writing it

      so it says
      I could be a truck

      this is the same
      this is the same

the dirt was warm, like a blanket

the *vqol*

the pirate of the wow
this is the constant of the flowing and the flower

      area expec-c-c seas

the special face
the other face
the nightshade face

I am the monster, and I eat light
the bright world is keeping us

the denver nuggets play basketball in hiking boots

you need that mirror to stare back, huh?

> *124132qa*
> *[p oy*
>> *—Odin C. M. N.*

I stood there in green pants
looking at green leaves

the soft green of north carolina ferns
the colder day with the whistles

to learn of the world thru books
the growling convenience

z-anything
gantry

flock to leap uncommon
umcobbem

the lightning bug octave

a good, blue car rolling
ninety and the night

the carpet in there was a green blowout
it was day two, and the song was stuck up there

alone or aloe
world worm three

this is the sky for now
using the laser numbers for that "wow"

work the sun, sunny
name something with colors and movement

this is the slight first world and enough thought
that could be the number one

earth is all right, ok?
this is the night of the other word

e, ex, err, earthward

spoom or spoon
the roger *galax*

basque art up high
front flip and baby paper

throw something into the hole
invisible pyramid when

that machine growing
I mean, *growling*

the sunshine cloud
or someone with arrows

the meaning of the eye
reading magazines at the supermarket

the thing in the woods is me

this is the word on the street on saturday morning

this is the flight of that color
to name it purple — oh, I get it

this is the brain walking
a friend of the sun

guess up big in the wheat
let's see our overlords

this good book of lightning
the old radio plaid

the cookbook pirate
earth is the mega

when the new clouds roll in
we will see that they are made of dreams

robot no rabbit

it lemoned out at miracle

this book is growling by now
looking for red ants

light head
no ware
thack fast
yes cool
time lock
yes yak
that that

æon books "on the hill"

eye milk

the words to understand this one
a succulent dish of mold

what is it, wolf?
when I become a rock

locked to the wall
       earth says, "no fits"

earth is expecting something
it's the wrong planet

are you still writing your book?
warthog (the spectral falls)

po box
pox

because I can't feel it

room for desert
(yes, one "s")

sand snail earthward
words and cotton ball earth, yet no spaces

that sound is the festooned *wet cetera*
earth is the ace

the start of a new dollar
when I become a bat

peppercorn earth shroud
why is "why" the word to grow with?

eat eyes
eating

II

889th & wadsworth

later rabbit
nothing I am wearing

this is normal

    earth needs some help
    let's call the aliens
    send a message with your mind
    they will hear it

        help us!
        help!

when I claim to be the *un*
am I really the *un-un*?

surfing bird here

the period of pencils
the period of the carolina wolf

the backwards gum I get
when I return with the brain

inside of the normal orb
what is water?

       this is a light
       tummy house

this is the outdoors version
the project with the worms

on the defensive side we want to make sure
and sort of control
the uh,   time of possession

you need a hum to get the beginning

a can of beans on the fire

to be called for the fork in the eye
a game with the blue pawn and *di-di-dah*

a language bird chirping
a frost giant

I've won this earth
I'm wording it this way

that is the aim of the learning center
to combine the stomach meats and learning

some coffee in the cabin
this building was once a pine tree

could be the sock and wheel
earth is the creature

charcoal

in the cloned forest
this is the other world of the people or persons

earth gets red and sore from waiting for so long
how long does it take to make a rock or two?

       earth makes rocks every day
       and waits for you to look at them

the worm is the same way
the better people

you are a cone
everything is a cone

something blue
this is the tunnel for low light

when I get back to wearing the crown
a limit of five this time

y. s.

the cartoon gamma

the pillow cake that talks
is that the fastest you've got?

      the tater fount
the flute, now

you've found the golden poem!
earth becomes the nightwood after eight

copper the one basic
not one penny for it

prove it to the bones
this is the program, ok?

the normal ice volunteer at all times

pell the pleff

o one is o
the proof of o (o saying o)

it was v or
the clue box soul

v is the ultra five
that lenny (one len)

the green dirt here
using words to write a poem

      nothing for now, thanks

a machine, alone at night
thinking of meat

the special time of the johnny carson

on *the tonight show* earth
learning in school and how is the johnny carson?

the final tree of the night and that earth word
word words

throwing salt was a plain deal kiss
the learning toy is sharpened this way

soon, cool anne
on that day there was a snow

an animal, or name something
a planet of monsters in the mud

"b" is a big brainpan

standing on the shore, I looked thru the stars
one was missing; I said nothing

    the ever-present now
    now is the now

    the little now
    the snowy now

on earth
it's tomorrow already

and now, the extended forecast with meteorologist, j. d. nelson
wow! it looks great out there, with temps in the 70s

starting to eat

seeking the blue
this is the blue
that older day
this later
one sets
that older one
this is the louie limit
this is barking brain
when I get back there
when I get the thumb again
this is the light time
room for it
hear this one now
you need to hear it
you need to listen
this is the friend of all
this merit of the coin
when flipping a dime

you are the sun in the restaurant biz

earth is rusting
(the metal trees)

it could be a false flavor
the clock ticking looks like a batch of biscuits

       the *steppy* sea

earth was the word
earth was all early

do you know the slow rope grower?
this is the first soil of the new earth

this is the period of the thunking love
this is the out-word and the up-word

wuh-wuh-wuh-wuh-wuh
sounds great, man!

whipple joints

a salad, perhaps
dallas about

sand *handwich* hank
what was it like eating the clouds?

this is the *gexx* — come on!
begging for tree life

needing sock work
needing food foot

when I was a plumber (but never was)
when I was a policeman in a felt suit

in my green fur
linus, minus the hat

to speak of clouds

here in the trees

this is the same thing all over the sun
this is a new pine tree

whenever it comes to something
dharma chalk

a blue jay calling for its friends
peanuts! peanuts!

never really a true green (we call it red)
they would rather have a salad

the blinking brain by itself
no one gets it

that sharp jark

the soap was an apple
the brain bucked

I was made for liking football
because of the noon

        mcdonald's at crossroads mall
        the slippery plastic booths

        the mood lighting
        salt crystals on golden fries

        the smell of the walgreens
        the miracle clam hat

the unit of the you
280 spruce st. tennis courts

the now of the now and now

lafayette
out on the prairie
       prairie sunshine
       blue sky cottonwoods

if this is the chain sauce
       the works

       wow! how
did you do that?

the first feature is the wolf
another life outfit

that song why
that long why
that sodden why
that salty what and why

       the green sky
       this is the weird why

the young hulk instinct

at long's iris gardens
knowing the known for nothing

this is the real-time lake map
next door to the home depot

the channel of the future
sports and the falcon voice

I know what you need to be the donkey
this is walking thru walls, all right

unit f (the train for chow and crown)
the other tea, a caldwell

dime or time

I was an electronic blip and bloop
call back with the potato of the ear

the green of the plants
break it, beaky or beale

earth is the medicine
earth is the hungry puppet

there was *this* before there was *this*
the proof of the control mechanism

who owns the meteor?
the people in the sky

stop doing something
how long is the *underlong*?

ox is ox (zero x)

thoughts for the crinkling sounds and that flipping
yes that roof is the world now
that would be something to say when I do think
later than the rope and back there
the word almost started with the incorrect letter (a)

thought for the sinking sounds and that fracking
yes that woof is the world new
that weed beef something to say when I don't think
laser and the *roke* and back there
the world almost started with the incorrect letter (k)

thog for sing sing sow and flat falcon
yessed that woo is woo new
that word bee something to say when I dew *thark*
laser and the robe and back hair
thee world almost starred with the incorrect laser (z)

learning to live in a cave

when I returned, I had a new brain
this is the typing of my new brain

it was house night with the tv shoe
I cut the table with the butter knife

another star
the fox, a weirdo with a sword

watch out for the lemon yellow
the first one is *wooo-hoooom*

across the aisle was a box of the new cheddar mix,
and I thought,

well, here is something the king cannot buy

standing there like a postage stamp

still in need of some sock work
no one weeps for the collapsed stars

this is the first paul stanley
this is the wall of canada

this is track & field at loaf 'n jug

this is the real tv light
I don't black out

this morning was a green lime puzzle
easily solved, for I love citrus

knuckles in there for the word to beep

the western world of the subdivision, circa 1979

the smart help is the merit of the bounce
be the smart helper

that old trouble and helping me with that help
that morning help

would you prefer the jazz station
or the lark of the wind?

stare at the sun with me
the lone merit and sleep for coal eyes

the church on the right

newark liberty, I guess

my hands are asleep as I type this
the sock of the tool bag

I sleep in the dirt
looking for cake

the truck and the one speaking
this is the trouble with wires

the alpha time & conditioning this sound

on the planet of never (here and there)
the hot foot is the good foot of the machine

the otter thought the other way
we forgot about the other clue

this would be the stomach and the fright
that's called my eye

shark
or was it *sharp*?

rat bacon
the wrong cooking

that that that

that
that
that

q. quiet

that wht
once a now
even three

back to paper
nu shts
g. grin

over spored
nevered
shout ax

it stock
like like
in trubb

start plasma
ever it
the nice

& why wee
the nevery
not very

baby unit
starting snz
exit rm

now eng
this tud
or

lookout bee
not yr evermind
slow ruck

noight innit
seven ft
owls out

hen row
tee rubby
water wht

the word is the forest and the pillow brook

oh, circling
the back fox

good light bull out

uncle clean wearing a sprinkler
needing a repair, steak-oh

      what's the occasion?

you were a blob yesterday?
well, I eat gold

I'm all over
down into the sun

start with the sun

room for it in '74
washington shoes will do

there was a big brushing when I woke up this morning
I started a new block of text

you were discovered so long ago that your *handbacks* are green

when I return with the window hands I will be the money king
learn of me and my wonderful money hands

would you like to do something else with the money?
yes, I would like to spend it on something nice for the children

ubber scrum the sandwich worm
never eaten one before

one mirror per level

which one is the war planet?
the one with the feathers

space camp was a dream for the kid
but no one could send him to another planet
so he stowed away on a space freighter
with a bag full of crackers
and small, steel cans of grape juice

nice metals for those who eat
be the priest eating sandals

earth needs a protein bar to show up naked

III

the basic sounds for your world

in the pockets
scenes in the daytime

orthogonal "e" / o. e. s.
redworld is another "r"

the chance to eat a butterfly
the first of the pesto, forthright

get your numbers on your own time
a triangle would make a great breakfast

I looked for the people in the convenience store
        but no one was there

alien memory foam

it was the other "r" / we rio
err, attractions with the ham name tag

"b" binder
l.w.q. car "a" at first

       therewith
       to know where we are

walk a mile point five
crake *veck*

statesville fishing first
the cardamom we

here we are, bathing in it
earth has many space friends

something for the red

this is the basic voice
using lights for the planets

the color of the moon
I remember the pastel ships in the night sky

spotless tomorrow spartacist
search party americanisms

lake louisville
grass clippings for a bed

receiving transmissions
sent from a friend of a friend

beyond any goog.
the continuation of the sparklin' harrisons

javelin bevin bunion versa delhi

is an "x" ok?
the book is not a fixed tree

the world is a cloud of paper
the power of the new milk

the sun is all paid for
you can sleep in a tent

we've been to mars
we've cracked earth eggs with giants

the world's like this
blue & wet

a breath of fresh earth

praying and writing and eating insects
I ate a cricket (or something)

your likeness on big money
so much space for humankind

I was asleep on a tree stump
startled awake by the sunlight

  where am I?

tamper-proof for you
receiving blocks of milk from space

words are coming out of the machine, like eels
squirming

naked in the hovercraft

in the rolling garden
picturing pike$ peak

a little of the orange fireside
it's free with bread

weber's hands foresting
don't wake the machine

descender atrophy
yes, the best cheddar

sequenced
overcharged for the light beam

everyone has the same lunch today:
peanut butter crackers

the radio horse

on the radio with lemon
making everybody squint

who is the metal dentist?
harp music in the forest

the binoculars are in the bag
we have snacks, like these apricots

the blackest of night in a jar on the shelf

the co-spidering stereo attack cactus from '82 is on display

garden hanging g-side to confuse the *uhh*
vic and voice, the challenge together for this piece

the rear of hiking
coming kitchen there

a place to eat the toast
there is power in the trees

the pea lea is a duggan
slow earth is proud of mary

chromed rice

it was a strange "e"
the sixth "x" with the moon and the sun

there I was, with a boy scout *fieldbook* and a butter knife

see me in the dark with glowing hands?
I'll return with the good bagels

the stones were moved by the original snowman
the best thing about having a third eye is being able to see
the red hubs

the sun-man

free gas
just sit on the moon)

uncomfortable & messy
this is the wild

    no one talks

a creature showing teeth
the skull wallet

the eye is away
part of the *xorne* error

incredibly, the stars were purple for a moment

this is a nature book

without any midnight
this is a confusing level

midnight shark, alone
in the middle of the ocean

justin of the language arts program
gauging the realm

owing hi "p" to loaf
yes, I have the tree in water

the red sheriff goes for the heart of the bull
going into the sun for the third time

earth is the medicine world

I like those train shows on pbs
I understand how dee retained the bat

after a number from the pond
this space of mind in the woods

rankings unto thee (street banking)
the monsters in the zoo are porous dream vessels

      western matters
      the chosen bull

      now for symbols
      clear lake today

the average face will appear in the mirror each morning

on a bed of *lettucized* bread

were you ever a duck in the muddy lake
quacking for crackers while floating

      making it look easy with your duck know-how?

disown hooks
to a bird, and in this case, the solar body

outside with the coyotes, squeezing under fences
the people are not eating chicken dinners

it'd better be a blank world with no problems

the red nanoseconds permeate

winter is on loan again
he'd l.l. around us

like the free world
in my msg tree

when the sun sets
it is easier to eat moss

legs wheeling
a circle of sunlight

waffle was up
the food is lenient

it requires a *crack!* to start

**the silent mouse was watching
and recording everything**

typing with these things on my hands
now I'm free

the most ominous thing you can build
name it!

no world in the water anymore
because the fish have left with the lions

seeing the sun made us weep

this whip & that

sleep for a week
the bing of the book when inherent

what is a stomach eye?
something you ate?

height restriction mandible
I pledge dots for the teeth

jack planet was a salad
I've been a muppet

free people from your time
earth has pirates, too

the oak lords, especially
be the bobcat of the old grove

the smoking gravy

was it a clone?
ears are but björn

major scale / kale
fracking for rabbits

typing on glass
one bishop was interested in math

see the pines?
the letter luck

the shape of the fixing crow
belief in the afterlife civilization

soon to be a blue wolf

is there anything in the trees?
a comedic shoe

      what more could you ask for?

      well, for one thing,
            could you please hold it down?

raisin bran breath
you are spidered enough to stand with the roots of the trees

relax and enjoy the stars

earth can be difficult for the explorer
sideways dreams at the equator

if geometry is the common language
and the sink is full of grapes

    what then?

an orange will surround itself with books
eat good meals to satisfy the herd

here in the blue space
it's almost *subset*

unpuppeted

this is the earth with no phone booths
how am I supposed to change into superman?

learning about the *goodwood*
a year of fresh desserts, please

too close to the sun
built for the speed of the world

in the world of sleep there is a magic cactus
obsessed with the space between spaces

I looked up to see something
it looked like me, floating above my house

it squints as it sits

into the brain we go
as a shrimp floats by in an *earthrobe*

a can of sand dreaming of soup
is that a real thing that people do?

      (most earthlings do)

a crawling insect yawn
the raw earth

yes, a dream
what if there were a room inside of this room?

good mood morning
it is time for sleep

      I have a head full of cats

Afterword

The title of this collection comes from a phrase from *The Cloud of Unknowing*, an anonymous work of Christian mysticism written in Middle English in the late 14th century. "In ghostly onehead" essentially means "in spiritual union" with the creative force of the universe. I have long felt that, as a writer, I act as a conduit through which this force flows.

My work is influenced by the Beat writers, especially Jack Kerouac's spontaneous prose technique, and the cut-up technique pioneered by William S. Burroughs. My writing is also influenced by Dada and Surrealism. Most of my poems are created through the cutting up and collaging of my own freewriting.

The 75 never-before-published poems in this collection were written over a period of exactly 2,000 days, from 23 July 2015 to 12 January 2021, in Lafayette, Colorado, USA.

—J. D. Nelson, December 2022

About the Author

J. D. Nelson was born on Saint Patrick's Day 1971 in Trenton, New Jersey. Since 2002, more than 2,000 of his poems have appeared internationally in more than 300 print and online publications. *in ghostly onehead* is Nelson's first full-length poetry collection. Visit his website, MadVerse.com, for more information and links to his published work. His haiku blog is at JDNelson.net. Nelson lives in Colorado.

Made in the USA
Las Vegas, NV
13 January 2023

65580549R00055